This journal belongs to

I HAVE LOVED Kahlil Gibran's *The Prophet* since I first read it many years ago. I consider it to be one of the most beautiful books ever written – and I am not alone. Gibran is one of the bestselling poets of all time with millions of copies of *The Prophet* sold since it was first published in 1923. Gibran's artworks, while less known, are equally beautiful. Their fluid spiritual energy honours both the human form and the divine spirit within and around us.

I wish to thank the Gibran National Committee for The Gibran Museum in Beirut, Lebanon for granting us license to publish the images featured herein and for their kind assistance in providing high-resolution scans of the original art works. The Gibran Museum is housed in the monastery Gibran purchased in 1926. After his death in 1931, he was buried in the hermitage there as per his wishes. The contents of Gibran's New York studio were moved there in 1932 and the monastery with his furniture, personal belongings, manuscripts and 440 original paintings were transformed into a museum in 1975.

It is with immense pleasure that I present forty-two of Gibran's paintings with excerpts from *The Prophet*. I personally chose the images and the quotes, and it is truly an honour and the realisation of a dream to share them with you here. I trust they will inspire, move and guide you as they have done me.

With love and light,
Toni Carmine Salerno

THEN THE GATES OF HIS HEART WERE FLUNG OPEN, AND HIS JOY FLEW FAR OVER THE SEA. AND HE CLOSED HIS EYES AND PRAYED IN THE SILENCES OF HIS SOUL.

When love beckons to you, follow him,
Though his ways are hard and steep.
And when his wings enfold you yield to him,
Though the sword hidden among his pinions may wound you.
And when he speaks to you believe in him,
Though his voice may shatter your dreams as the north wind lays
waste the garden.

LOVE GIVES NAUGHT BUT ITSELF AND TAKES NAUGHT BUT FROM ITSELF.
LOVE POSSESSES NOT NOR WOULD IT BE POSSESSED;
FOR LOVE IS SUFFICIENT UNTO LOVE.
WHEN YOU LOVE YOU SHOULD NOT SAY, "GOD IS IN MY HEART,"
BUT RATHER, "I AM IN THE HEART OF GOD."
AND THINK NOT YOU CAN DIRECT THE COURSE OF LOVE, FOR LOVE,
IF IT FINDS YOU WORTHY, DIRECTS YOUR COURSE.

Love has no other desire but to fulfill itself.
But if you love and must needs have desires, let these be your desires:
To melt and be like a running brook that sings its melody to the night.
To know the pain of too much tenderness.
To be wounded by your own understanding of love;
And to bleed willingly and joyfully.
To wake at dawn with a winged heart and
give thanks for another day of loving;
To rest at the noon hour and meditate love's ecstasy;
To return home at eventide with gratitude;
And then to sleep with a prayer for the beloved in your heart
and a song of praise upon your lips.

BUT LET THERE BE SPACES IN YOUR TOGETHERNESS.
AND LET THE WINDS OF THE HEAVENS DANCE BETWEEN YOU.
LOVE ONE ANOTHER, BUT MAKE NOT A BOND OF LOVE:
LET IT RATHER BE A MOVING SEA BETWEEN THE SHORES OF YOUR SOULS.

GIVE YOUR HEARTS, BUT NOT INTO EACH OTHER'S KEEPING.
FOR ONLY THE HAND OF LIFE CAN CONTAIN YOUR HEARTS.
AND STAND TOGETHER YET NOT TOO NEAR TOGETHER:
FOR THE PILLARS OF THE TEMPLE STAND APART,
AND THE OAK TREE AND THE CYPRESS GROW NOT IN EACH OTHER'S SHADOW.

YOUR CHILDREN ARE NOT YOUR CHILDREN.
THEY ARE THE SONS AND DAUGHTERS OF LIFE'S LONGING FOR ITSELF.
THEY COME THROUGH YOU BUT NOT FROM YOU,
AND THOUGH THEY ARE WITH YOU YET THEY BELONG NOT TO YOU.
YOU MAY GIVE THEM YOUR LOVE BUT NOT YOUR THOUGHTS,
FOR THEY HAVE THEIR OWN THOUGHTS.
YOU MAY HOUSE THEIR BODIES BUT NOT THEIR SOULS,
FOR THEIR SOULS DWELL IN THE HOUSE OF TOMORROW,
WHICH YOU CANNOT VISIT, NOT EVEN IN YOUR DREAMS.
YOU MAY STRIVE TO BE LIKE THEM, BUT SEEK NOT TO MAKE THEM LIKE YOU.

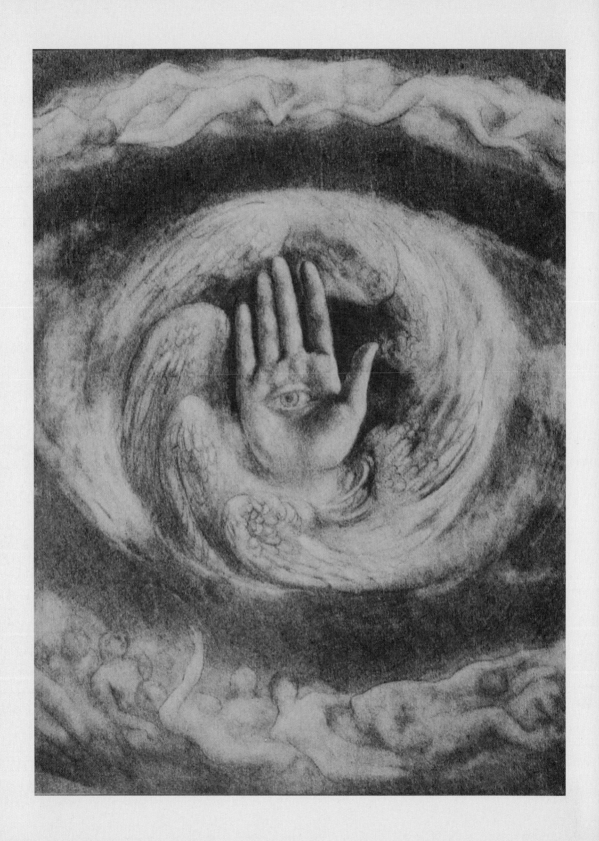

YOU GIVE BUT LITTLE WHEN YOU GIVE OF YOUR POSSESSIONS.
IT IS WHEN YOU GIVE OF YOURSELF THAT YOU TRULY GIVE.

IT IS WELL TO GIVE WHEN ASKED, BUT IT IS BETTER TO GIVE UNASKED,
THROUGH UNDERSTANDING;
AND TO THE OPEN-HANDED THE SEARCH FOR ONE WHO SHALL RECEIVE
IS JOY GREATER THAN GIVING.

AND WHEN YOU CRUSH AN APPLE WITH YOUR TEETH, SAY TO IT IN YOUR HEART:
"YOUR SEEDS SHALL LIVE IN MY BODY,
AND THE BUDS OF YOUR TOMORROW SHALL BLOSSOM IN MY HEART,
AND YOUR FRAGRANCE SHALL BE MY BREATH,
AND TOGETHER WE SHALL REJOICE THROUGH ALL THE SEASONS."

AND IN THE AUTUMN, WHEN YOU GATHER THE GRAPES OF YOUR VINEYARDS FOR
THE WINEPRESS, SAY IN YOUR HEART:
"I TOO AM A VINEYARD, AND MY FRUIT SHALL BE GATHERED FOR THE WINEPRESS,
AND LIKE NEW WINE I SHALL BE KEPT IN ETERNAL VESSELS."

AND IN WINTER, WHEN YOU DRAW THE WINE, LET THERE BE IN
YOUR HEART A SONG FOR EACH CUP;
AND LET THERE BE IN THE SONG A REMEMBRANCE FOR THE
AUTUMN DAYS, AND FOR THE VINEYARD, AND FOR THE WINEPRESS.

AND WHEN YOU WORK WITH LOVE YOU BIND YOURSELF TO
YOURSELF, AND TO ONE ANOTHER, AND TO GOD.

AND WHAT IS IT TO WORK WITH LOVE?
IT IS TO WEAVE THE CLOTH WITH THREADS DRAWN FROM YOUR HEART,
EVEN AS IF YOUR BELOVED WERE TO WEAR THAT CLOTH.

YOUR JOY IS YOUR SORROW UNMASKED.

WHEN YOU ARE JOYOUS, LOOK DEEP INTO YOUR HEART AND YOU SHALL FIND IT IS
ONLY THAT WHICH HAS GIVEN YOU SORROW THAT IS GIVING YOU JOY.

WHEN YOU ARE SORROWFUL, LOOK AGAIN IN YOUR HEART, AND YOU SHALL SEE THAT IN TRUTH YOU ARE WEEPING FOR THAT WHICH HAS BEEN YOUR DELIGHT.

SOME OF YOU SAY, "JOY IS GREATER THAN SORROW,"
AND OTHERS SAY, "NAY, SORROW IS THE GREATER."
BUT I SAY UNTO YOU, THEY ARE INSEPARABLE.

AND FORGET NOT THAT THE EARTH DELIGHTS TO FEEL YOUR
BARE FEET AND THE WINDS LONG TO PLAY WITH YOUR HAIR.

TO YOU THE EARTH YIELDS HER FRUIT, AND YOU SHALL NOT
WANT IF YOU BUT KNOW HOW TO FILL YOUR HANDS.

For the master spirit of the earth shall not sleep peacefully upon the wind till the needs of the least of you are satisfied.

YOU SHALL BE FREE INDEED WHEN YOUR DAYS ARE NOT WITHOUT
A CARE NOR YOUR NIGHTS WITHOUT A WANT AND A GRIEF,
BUT RATHER WHEN THESE THINGS GIRDLE YOUR LIFE AND YET
YOU RISE ABOVE THEM NAKED AND UNBOUND.

AND HOW SHALL YOU RISE BEYOND YOUR DAYS AND NIGHTS UNLESS
YOU BREAK THE CHAINS WHICH YOU AT THE DAWN OF YOUR
UNDERSTANDING HAVE FASTENED AROUND YOUR NOON HOUR?

YOUR SOUL IS OFTENTIMES A BATTLEFIELD, UPON WHICH YOUR REASON
AND YOUR JUDGMENT WAGE WAR AGAINST YOUR PASSION AND YOUR APPETITE.
WOULD THAT I COULD BE THE PEACEMAKER IN YOUR SOUL, THAT I MIGHT TURN
THE DISCORD AND THE RIVALRY OF YOUR ELEMENTS INTO ONENESS AND MELODY.

AMONG THE HILLS, WHEN YOU SIT IN THE COOL SHADE OF THE WHITE POPLARS,
SHARING THE PEACE AND SERENITY OF DISTANT FIELDS AND MEADOWS –
THEN LET YOUR HEART SAY IN SILENCE, "GOD RESTS IN REASON."
AND WHEN THE STORM COMES, AND THE MIGHTY WIND SHAKES THE FOREST,
AND THUNDER AND LIGHTNING PROCLAIM THE MAJESTY OF THE SKY, –
THEN LET YOUR HEART SAY IN AWE, "GOD MOVES IN PASSION."
AND SINCE YOU ARE A BREATH IN GOD'S SPHERE, AND A LEAF IN GOD'S FOREST,
YOU TOO SHOULD REST IN REASON AND MOVE IN PASSION.

YOUR PAIN IS THE BREAKING OF THE SHELL THAT ENCLOSES
YOUR UNDERSTANDING.
EVEN AS THE STONE OF THE FRUIT MUST BREAK, THAT ITS HEART MAY STAND IN
THE SUN, SO MUST YOU KNOW PAIN.
AND COULD YOU KEEP YOUR HEART IN WONDER AT THE DAILY MIRACLES OF
YOUR LIFE, YOUR PAIN WOULD NOT SEEM LESS WONDROUS THAN YOUR JOY;
AND YOU WOULD ACCEPT THE SEASONS OF YOUR HEART, EVEN AS YOU HAVE
ALWAYS ACCEPTED THE SEASONS THAT PASS OVER YOUR FIELDS.

YOUR HEARTS KNOW IN SILENCE THE SECRETS OF THE DAYS AND THE NIGHTS.

AND SEEK NOT THE DEPTHS OF YOUR KNOWLEDGE WITH STAFF
OR SOUNDING LINE.
FOR SELF IS A SEA BOUNDLESS AND MEASURELESS.
SAY NOT, "I HAVE FOUND THE TRUTH," BUT RATHER, "I HAVE FOUND A TRUTH."
SAY NOT, "I HAVE FOUND THE PATH OF THE SOUL."
SAY RATHER, "I HAVE MET THE SOUL WALKING UPON MY PATH."
FOR THE SOUL WALKS UPON ALL PATHS.
THE SOUL WALKS NOT UPON A LINE, NEITHER DOES IT GROW LIKE A REED.
THE SOUL UNFOLDS ITSELF, LIKE A LOTUS OF COUNTLESS PETALS.

NO MAN CAN REVEAL TO YOU AUGHT BUT THAT WHICH ALREADY LIES
HALF ASLEEP IN THE DAWNING OF YOUR KNOWLEDGE.

THE TEACHER WHO WALKS IN THE SHADOW OF THE TEMPLE, AMONG HIS
FOLLOWERS, GIVES NOT OF HIS WISDOM BUT RATHER OF HIS FAITH
AND HIS LOVINGNESS.
IF HE IS INDEED WISE HE DOES NOT BID YOU ENTER THE HOUSE OF HIS WISDOM,
BUT RATHER LEADS YOU TO THE THRESHOLD OF YOUR OWN MIND.

THE ASTRONOMER MAY SPEAK TO YOU OF HIS UNDERSTANDING OF SPACE,
BUT HE CANNOT GIVE YOU HIS UNDERSTANDING.

THE MUSICIAN MAY SING TO YOU OF THE RHYTHM WHICH IS IN ALL SPACE,
BUT HE CANNOT GIVE YOU THE EAR WHICH ARRESTS THE RHYTHM,
NOR THE VOICE THAT ECHOES IT.

AND EVEN AS EACH ONE OF YOU STANDS ALONE IN GOD'S KNOWLEDGE,
SO MUST EACH ONE OF YOU BE ALONE IN HIS KNOWLEDGE OF GOD
AND IN HIS UNDERSTANDING OF THE EARTH.

YOUR FRIEND IS YOUR NEEDS ANSWERED.

AND LET THERE BE NO PURPOSE IN FRIENDSHIP
SAVE THE DEEPENING OF THE SPIRIT.

AND LET YOUR BEST BE FOR YOUR FRIEND.

IF HE MUST KNOW THE EBB OF YOUR TIDE, LET HIM KNOW ITS FLOOD ALSO.
FOR WHAT IS YOUR FRIEND THAT YOU SHOULD SEEK HIM WITH HOURS TO KILL?
SEEK HIM ALWAYS WITH HOURS TO LIVE.

FOR IN THE DEW OF LITTLE THINGS THE HEART
FINDS ITS MORNING AND IS REFRESHED.

You talk when you cease to be at peace with your thoughts;
And when you can no longer dwell in the solitude of your heart you
live in your lips, and sound is a diversion and a pastime.

Of time you would make a stream upon whose bank
you would sit and watch its flowing.
Yet the timeless in you is aware of life's timelessness,
And knows that yesterday is but today's memory and
tomorrow is today's dream.

AND THAT WHICH SINGS AND CONTEMPLATES IN YOU IS STILL DWELLING WITHIN
THE BOUNDS OF THAT FIRST MOMENT WHICH SCATTERED THE STARS INTO SPACE.

WHO AMONG YOU DOES NOT FEEL THAT HIS POWER TO LOVE IS BOUNDLESS?

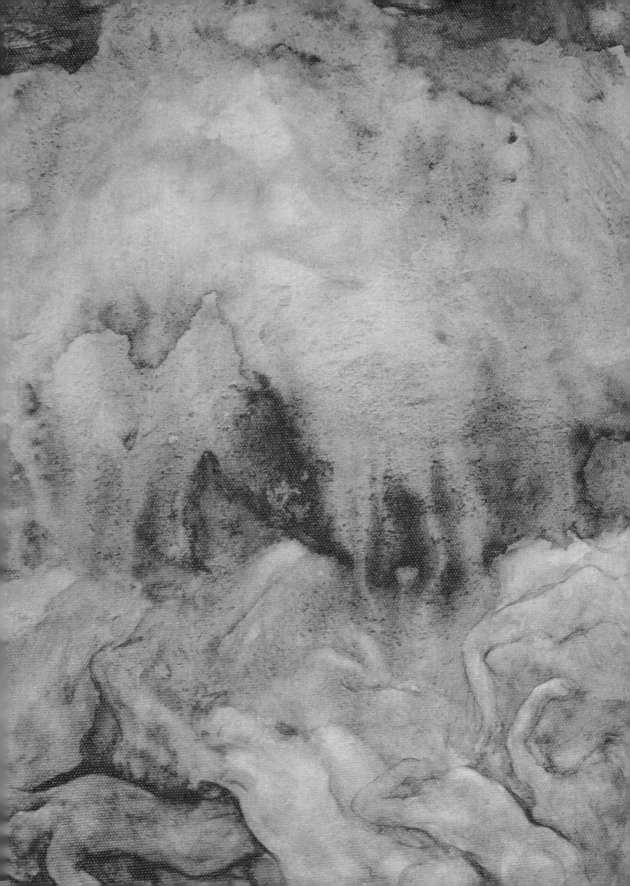

But if in your thought you must measure time into
seasons, let each season encircle all the other seasons,
And let today embrace the past with remembrance and
the future with longing.

OF THE GOOD IN YOU I CAN SPEAK, BUT NOT OF THE EVIL.
FOR WHAT IS EVIL BUT GOOD TORTURED BY ITS OWN HUNGER AND THIRST?

SURELY THE FRUIT CANNOT SAY TO THE ROOT,
"BE LIKE ME, RIPE AND FULL AND EVER GIVING OF YOUR ABUNDANCE."
FOR TO THE FRUIT GIVING IS A NEED, AS RECEIVING IS A NEED TO THE ROOT.

You pray in your distress and in your need; would that you might pray also in the fullness of your joy and in your days of abundance. For what is prayer but the expansion of your self into the living ether?

And if it is for your comfort to pour your darkness into space, it is also for your delight to pour forth the dawning of your heart.

WHEN YOU PRAY YOU RISE TO MEET IN THE AIR THOSE WHO ARE PRAYING AT
THAT VERY HOUR, AND WHOM SAVE IN PRAYER YOU MAY NOT MEET.

I cannot teach you how to pray in words.
God listens not to your words save when
He Himself utters them through your lips.
And I cannot teach you the prayer of the seas
and the forests and the mountains.
But you who are born of the mountains and the forests
and the seas can find their prayer in your heart,
And if you but listen in the stillness of the night
you shall hear them saying in silence:
"Our God, who art our winged self, it is thy will in us that willeth.
"It is thy desire in us that desireth.
"It is thy urge in us that would turn our nights,
which are thine, into days, which are thine also.
"We cannot ask thee for aught, for thou knowest
our needs before they are born in us:
"Thou art our need; and in giving us more of thyself thou givest
us all."

AND YOUR BODY IS THE HARP OF YOUR SOUL,
AND IT IS YOURS TO BRING FORTH SWEET MUSIC FROM IT OR CONFUSED SOUNDS.

GO TO YOUR FIELDS AND YOUR GARDENS, AND YOU SHALL LEARN THAT IT IS THE
PLEASURE OF THE BEE TO GATHER HONEY OF THE FLOWER,
BUT IT IS ALSO THE PLEASURE OF THE FLOWER TO YIELD ITS HONEY TO THE BEE.
FOR TO THE BEE A FLOWER IS A FOUNTAIN OF LIFE,
AND TO THE FLOWER A BEE IS A MESSENGER OF LOVE,
AND TO BOTH, BEE AND FLOWER, THE GIVING AND THE RECEIVING OF PLEASURE
IS A NEED AND AN ECSTASY.

WHERE SHALL YOU SEEK BEAUTY, AND HOW SHALL YOU FIND
HER UNLESS SHE HERSELF BE YOUR WAY AND YOUR GUIDE?

BEAUTY IS ETERNITY GAZING AT ITSELF IN A MIRROR.
BUT YOU ARE ETERNITY AND YOU ARE THE MIRROR.

... BEAUTY IS LIFE WHEN LIFE UNVEILS HER HOLY FACE.

YOUR DAILY LIFE IS YOUR TEMPLE AND YOUR RELIGION.
WHENEVER YOU ENTER INTO IT TAKE WITH YOU YOUR ALL.

AND IF YOU WOULD KNOW GOD, BE NOT THEREFORE A SOLVER OF RIDDLES.
RATHER LOOK ABOUT YOU AND YOU SHALL SEE HIM
PLAYING WITH YOUR CHILDREN.
AND LOOK INTO SPACE; YOU SHALL SEE HIM WALKING IN THE CLOUD,
OUTSTRETCHING HIS ARMS IN THE LIGHTNING AND DESCENDING IN RAIN.
YOU SHALL SEE HIM SMILING IN FLOWERS,
THEN RISING AND WAVING HIS HANDS IN TREES.

FOR LIFE AND DEATH ARE ONE, EVEN AS THE RIVER AND THE SEA ARE ONE.

IN THE DEPTH OF YOUR HOPES AND DESIRES
LIES YOUR SILENT KNOWLEDGE OF THE BEYOND;
AND LIKE SEEDS DREAMING BENEATH THE
SNOW YOUR HEART DREAMS OF SPRING.
TRUST THE DREAMS, FOR IN THEM IS HIDDEN THE GATE TO ETERNITY.

FOR WHAT IS IT TO DIE BUT TO STAND NAKED IN THE WIND
AND TO MELT INTO THE SUN?

AND WHAT IS IT TO CEASE BREATHING BUT TO FREE THE BREATH FROM ITS
RESTLESS TIDES, THAT IT MAY RISE AND EXPAND AND SEEK GOD UNENCUMBERED?

ONLY WHEN YOU DRINK FROM THE RIVER OF SILENCE SHALL YOU INDEED SING.

WE WANDERERS, EVER SEEKING THE LONELIER WAY, BEGIN NO DAY WHERE WE
HAVE ENDED ANOTHER DAY; AND NO SUNRISE FINDS US WHERE SUNSET LEFT US.
EVEN WHILE THE EARTH SLEEPS WE TRAVEL.

WE ARE THE SEEDS OF THE TENACIOUS PLANT, AND IT IS IN OUR RIPENESS AND
OUR FULLNESS OF HEART THAT WE ARE GIVEN TO THE WIND
AND ARE SCATTERED.

Brief were my days among you, and briefer still the words
I have spoken.
But should my voice fade in your ears, and my love vanish
in your memory, then I will come again,
And with a richer heart and lips more yielding to the spirit
will I speak.

YEA, I SHALL RETURN WITH THE TIDE,
AND THOUGH DEATH MAY HIDE ME, AND THE GREATER SILENCE
ENFOLD ME, YET AGAIN WILL I SEEK YOUR UNDERSTANDING.
AND NOT IN VAIN WILL I SEEK.

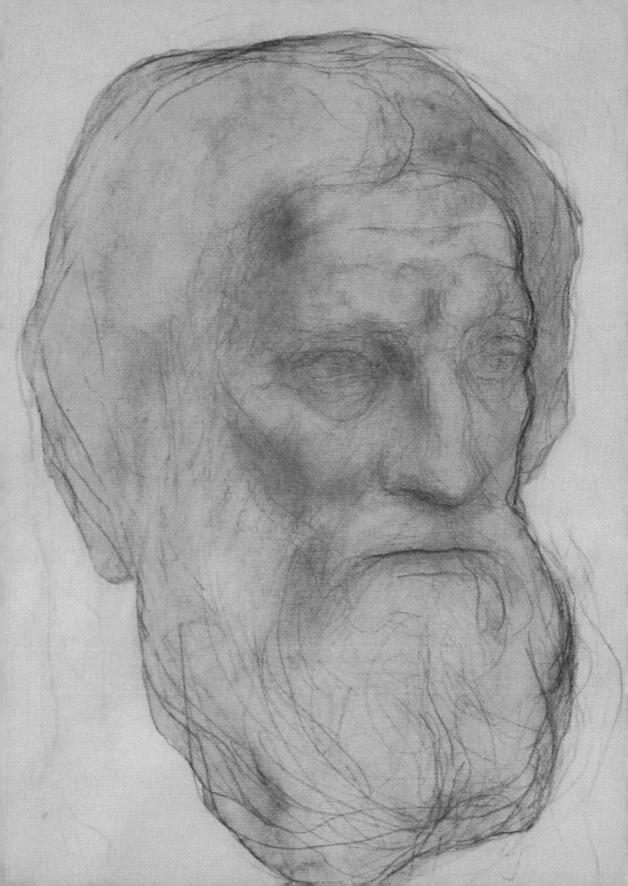

MAN'S NEEDS CHANGE, BUT NOT HIS LOVE, NOR HIS DESIRE
THAT HIS LOVE SHOULD SATISFY HIS NEEDS.

KNOW, THEREFORE, THAT FROM THE GREATER SILENCE I SHALL RETURN.

THE MIST THAT DRIFTS AWAY AT DAWN, LEAVING BUT DEW IN THE FIELDS,
SHALL RISE AND GATHER INTO A CLOUD AND THEN FALL DOWN IN RAIN.
AND NOT UNLIKE THE MIST HAVE I BEEN.

In the stillness of the night I have walked in your streets, and my spirit has entered your houses, And your heartbeats were in my heart, and your breath was upon my face, and I knew you all.

AYE, I KNEW YOUR JOY AND YOUR PAIN, AND IN YOUR SLEEP
YOUR DREAMS WERE MY DREAMS.

YOU HAVE BEEN TOLD THAT, EVEN LIKE A CHAIN,
YOU ARE AS WEAK AS YOUR WEAKEST LINK.
THIS IS BUT HALF THE TRUTH.
YOU ARE ALSO AS STRONG AS YOUR STRONGEST LINK.

TO MEASURE YOU BY YOUR SMALLEST DEED IS TO RECKON
THE POWER OF OCEAN BY THE FRAILTY OF ITS FOAM.

TO JUDGE YOU BY YOUR FAILURES IS TO CAST BLAME UPON
THE SEASONS FOR THEIR INCONSTANCY.

Ay, you are like an ocean,
And though heavy-grounded ships await the tide upon your
shores, yet, even like an ocean, you cannot hasten your tides.
And like the seasons you are also,
And though in your winter you deny your spring,
Yet spring, reposing within you,
smiles in her drowsiness and is not offended.

THINK NOT I SAY THESE THINGS IN ORDER THAT
YOU MAY SAY THE ONE TO THE OTHER,
"HE PRAISED US WELL.
"HE SAW BUT THE GOOD IN US."
I ONLY SPEAK TO YOU IN WORDS OF THAT WHICH YOU
YOURSELVES KNOW IN THOUGHT.

AND WHAT IS WORD KNOWLEDGE BUT A SHADOW OF WORDLESS KNOWLEDGE?
YOUR THOUGHTS AND MY WORDS ARE WAVES FROM A SEALED MEMORY THAT
KEEPS RECORDS OF OUR YESTERDAYS,
AND OF THE ANCIENT DAYS WHEN THE EARTH KNEW NOT US NOR HERSELF,
AND OF NIGHTS WHEN EARTH WAS UPWROUGHT WITH CONFUSION.

AND BEHOLD I HAVE FOUND THAT WHICH IS GREATER THAN WISDOM.
IT IS A FLAME SPIRIT IN YOU EVER GATHERING MORE OF ITSELF...

THESE MOUNTAINS AND PLAINS ARE A CRADLE AND A STEPPING-STONE.

WHENEVER YOU PASS BY THE FIELD WHERE YOU HAVE LAID YOUR ANCESTORS LOOK WELL THEREUPON, AND YOU SHALL SEE YOURSELVES AND YOUR CHILDREN DANCING HAND IN HAND.

YOU HAVE GIVEN ME MY DEEPER THIRSTING AFTER LIFE.
SURELY THERE IS NO GREATER GIFT TO A MAN THAN THAT WHICH TURNS
ALL HIS AIMS INTO PARCHING LIPS AND ALL LIFE INTO A FOUNTAIN.

AND IN THIS LIES MY HONOUR AND MY REWARD –
THAT WHENEVER I COME TO THE FOUNTAIN TO DRINK I FIND
THE LIVING WATER ITSELF THIRSTY;
AND IT DRINKS ME WHILE I DRINK IT.

YOU GIVE MUCH AND KNOW NOT THAT YOU GIVE AT ALL.

BUT THE HUNTER WAS ALSO THE HUNTED;
FOR MANY OF MY ARROWS LEFT MY BOW ONLY TO SEEK MY OWN BREAST.

AND I THE BELIEVER WAS ALSO THE DOUBTER...

THE STREAM HAS REACHED THE SEA, AND ONCE MORE THE GREAT
MOTHER HOLDS HER SON AGAINST HER BREAST.

FORGET NOT THAT I SHALL COME BACK TO YOU.
A LITTLE WHILE, AND MY LONGING SHALL GATHER DUST
AND FOAM FOR ANOTHER BODY.
A LITTLE WHILE, A MOMENT OF REST UPON THE WIND,
AND ANOTHER WOMAN SHALL BEAR ME.
FAREWELL TO YOU AND THE YOUTH I HAVE SPENT WITH YOU.
IT WAS BUT YESTERDAY WE MET IN A DREAM.

IF IN THE TWILIGHT OF MEMORY WE SHOULD MEET ONCE MORE, WE SHALL SPEAK
AGAIN TOGETHER AND YOU SHALL SING TO ME A DEEPER SONG.
AND IF OUR HANDS SHOULD MEET IN ANOTHER DREAM
WE SHALL BUILD ANOTHER TOWER IN THE SKY.

So saying he made a signal to the seamen, and straightaway
they weighed anchor and cast the ship loose from its
moorings, and they moved eastward.
And a cry came from the people as from a single heart,
and it rose into the dusk and was carried out over the sea
like a great trumpeting.
Only Almitra was silent, gazing after the ship until it had
vanished into the mist.
And when all the people were dispersed she still stood alone
upon the sea-wall, remembering in her heart his saying:
"A little while, a moment of rest upon the wind,
and another woman shall bear me."